red | book poems

asalott

phoenix surrenders to red
(blood | flames)
& is released.

purified
& offered
new life.

moon (body)

moon needs facelift.
sweeping clouds strip
craterous zits
with sifter & fang.
moon needs tummy tuck.
metallic winds slice
bulge, lunar tits
& luminous lard.
moon needs botox.
styrofoam cup
sparkle mouths shut
tingle ember burn
words absent.
no observations left.
a posteriori : single
synthesized moon
tries mingling
with the stars.

tongue (track)

- -

.track leads out a
town through forest
red metal rust
savory wet dirt

- -

in costumes & cream paint
we carry small branches
mallets that strike
rails become bells salivating melody

- -

lemon lime leaves
dead on hard ground
anticipate ice to enter
warm worm gums

- -

blue paint drips
we leave masks behind
oily phosphoric rainbows
rail becomes canvas as face melts

- -

white rime forms on copper
glitter in gravel
beacons of moonlight
play hide & seek on our tongue.

- -

music (cycles)

there is a miniature theater surrounded by
fire trucks & warehouses. lips pucker cigarettes,
sophisticated slobs in a swarming mass together,
but separate.

inside the theater radiates. superimposed
photographs projected on white globes
suspended from the ceiling. music is diverging
choices of various magnitude & timbre:
tangled arterial voices seized in pulsing cycles,
rhythms that swing back harrowing nights,
the taste of mucus & salt freezing on raw nostrils.

inside the walls buckle. a seething home for
bugged minds to mesmerize & feed on other
minds. antithesis & perception, to gather
the skirt of objection & meld it like rot iron.

music as reality: flowing river of sounds & rests.
each voice its own pattern, each pattern its own
turn in an infinite manipulation of light | sound
that forge together sensible qualities
in the spark of one mind.

child (box)

emerald leaves on crimson apple trees
in the backyard.
white shudders on blue house.
green onions for chewing.
orange pumpkins buried
in the garden
by the shedding cottonwoods.
simple & smooth links.
metallic scent of chain
on dirty hands.
sky high swings
powered by short limbs,
my boyish legs
that found their way.
my chubby pink fingers
that discovered their secrets.
sanded & smooth
like piano keys:
a wooden cigar box
filled with ticket stubs,
rocks, miniatures, letters,
figurines, bottle rockets
never to be lit,
poems
never to be read.

circus (tent)

girl lit a fag in the fog & darkness. her name was
unimportant. tight rope artists & red balloons fangs of
cobras rising from baskets loud gongs sweet smoke
pouring out tent flaps of meat on bone, she weaved
through flesh. i took quick steps to catch up.
i wandered into an open tent & discovered new smells.
sweet vinegar fermented milk & baklava new people
like hunters & prey new art like graffiti & melting glass
new sights like death & delicate feasts of grease. she
found me & we went deeper into the tent. then we
were severed.
i was pushed in this room where i ran into a woman
her name was too important like love too serious like
sex too momentary. new silk cloth new water like
mead she was peppermint & nicotine grass & cologne
a mixture of everything & nothing, she lead me into
darkness. not alone. there were fireflies & clouds.
the circus (tent) in the distance. flames sparked up
through the brush. dancing skin tight bodies flickered
drum beats beads of sweat breaking apart evaporating
in the heat.
suddenly she disappeared into the forest
further into abyss.
i'm disoriented now.
the night is thick. there is a stream close by, the wind
stench of fish. overgrowth grabs my legs wet moss
slapping my face no light no hand to hold branches
twisted like snakes somber tears scent of earth the
moon orange & bright, it guides me
back to the circus (tent).
i take quick steps
to catch up.

brain (lunch)

brain (lunch)
left in the sun.
peanut butter & jelly
abandoned for the bus?
apartment doors dilapidated
from police raids on meth labs.
soggy unidentified contents   in a
swollen brown bag. wet on the corners,
resting on the stairs. leaving a wet mark
like a sweaty brain on the concrete step.
placed delicately, waiting   for someone
to return home &   become a zombie.

dragonfly requiem

we collide in florida. ten of us
on a mildewed patio, filleted
across a warped green table;
sweating, drinking, serving.

we (the apostle's children) are alive.
my brother plays piano- a requiem
for the ping pong ball that bounces
as competitive jaws harp.

my friends laugh, vodka sodden clowns,
harder than they've ever laughed before.
they make balloon animals
and pop them with their fingernails.

i sit in the rain, a lawn ornament.
smoking to feel alone.
dragonflies skim the lake
in separate infinite paths,
a pilgrimage to the sky.

our prayers collide & the dragonflies
carry them up to a spider's web,
where they wait to be digested
by a spider who's long been dead.

red wine & candle wax

11:11am
watch the birds at play. see how their mouths
clip sunbathers secrets & spread them across
the beach. what large nudes expand vermillion
flanks to the sun god, gather rays to flake skin.
old thighs peek & dive from mountain water.
watch the movement of a day toss fast around
your resting place. see how innocent the people
are, listen to the senseless drabble: planes pierce
the gutted ears, familiar echoes of something wet.
3:33pm
soggy florescent orange chips create rings of
moisture- a once late night snack turned
aside the creek. a sandal left stranded by a tuber,
stuck in the rocks, steers water to its procession.
humdrum buzz of a summer day is a black tube
half-inflated. it sits & waits, there to replace the
one i stole from the same shore yesterday.
10:10pm
monotony. same night. repeated & repeated.
summer solstice full moon remedy. cops
knocking on every door, climbing through the
window cracks, listening to this conversation.
tree shadows move across the street like blimps.
monotony. same night, only slight difference.
maybe tonight, red wine.

12:12am
tv lights flicker, disintegrate off the pink walls
of your house. someone's chopping inside.
a midnight meal. there are people that watch
the tiny blue bulbs of light & there are those
that refuse to drive miniature cars into a traffic
jam, smoke the white noise from black screens.
anorexic leaves on your doorstep gnaw sidewalk,
hide behind clipped fashion magazines.
both frail configurations of death. you kick them
across the carpet, but as ashes they cling & hide.
when you start the vacuum, they pose
as dust on your books.
1:11am
maybe humans are interviewing
like the dinosaurs & the others before them.
the earth is trying us out. soon it will eat us alive
& send us spinning into another god's
psyche. i chain smoke on the porch.
you converse in the window.
i worry about jobs, cars, school-
things i don't need or want.
2:22am
could we fall onto the bridge of a candle flame
& cross into a world in which our books
& knowledge mean nothing?
(suddenly everything we thought we knew
is gone. the theories of man
left motionless & wrong).

wings

| disconnected | trains shout cacophonous
proverbs | the rain is here | wood puddles the
black reflection of the sky | a dull actor | the
fabrication of ourselves | pixilated on surfaces. |
shallow depthless exterior | superficial outward
cover| i sip air from a rivulet on your neck |
i see lights in the trees | outside the walls | of
this house. | discordant euphoria | drops down |
like the silent fastening of wings |to our fossilized
backs   :|:   flight | static in midair. | around &
round these lights become figures | wayfarers of
electrical storms | trapped | bouncing off the
hollow | apartment complex. | they talk in
sparks | roman candles | indecipherable
languages. | limited to weight of my bones |
pulsing gravity in tendons | daunting freedom |
seems unreachable. |
i intend to be a dragon | a bird | or a fly. | us
two legged creatures | we climb | the mountain
to pray | meditate on the collision of rocks that
stretch out beyond vision. | the places we can
never touch |
without

wings.

sand monkeys

BAIL out of high tower wastelands! GO!
LIVE out as sand monkeys! SCAVENGE for
food in the lower canopy at the edge of a desert.
TRY to FIND dune god on a cloud, bouncing
from neurons, the oneness. DELIBERATE
when you need water, but ACT as if alone.
BECOME sand pirates: bandanas, shields,
goggles, gummy bears, sugar cubes... (sand wall
shoots vertical out of the creek bed, bristled wind
flattens the high towers, the stores, the people...)
CLIMB the avalanche as a desert bug. DIG on
all sixes, then TOPPLE down into lucid
debauchery. into a menacing beloved sand trap.
can't LET yourself SLIP deeper into the warm
grasp next to the water & shade. PUSH on- there
is no way but up. CLIMB to the edge, to the
furthest reaches of beasts & our absurd search for
god. numb legs automatic creatures of their own
ENTER the stage of the perpetual mind game:
LIE in the dust that becomes sky, liquid polish
motion & rhythm. POSE for a picture.
BATHE in pure awe.
this is god!
we FOUND the bitch.

printer | mass grave

it is like us to write words on paper.
destroy trees
to write these bad,
simple words.
& what more
poets leave extra   space
as if to say
our words
are worth
another branch.

trees write stories in their own skin
& we write ours over top,
drown out the grain of centuries
with blood ink.
to think if we sketched
the fabric of conscious thought
into our own skin.
alas. we create life
in the wake of their death.
to redeem this heinous act
against our oldest removed sisters
who exchange lung shit for oxygen
we propel our brains to create & destroy
in attempt to mimic nature & capture
the tragedy
of a fallen forest.

to take as much away

(as if copying a burning manuscript)

i knew i shouldn't have lit that cigarette
while i was sleep walking,
but i was dreaming about you.
this time you understood
my childhood obsession
with your intense blue eyes
& long thick lashes;
your desire to be eccentric
to the point of aggression.
& when i woke with drops of mourning
in the crest of my newly burnt eyelids:
i tried to squeeze darkness back into them,
reprint the genetic mockup of the dream,
manipulate you like ladders,
pick the parts of soul to rip,
the ones that were rightfully mine.
i tried to paste our mouths together
at the edges of the frame,
but my lips touched nothing.
sunrise sucked tight the last image
of your fresh tattoos, such a violent return
to consciousness & a blistered eye:
you’re a thousand miles away,
you've been gone twelve years,
& you never knew
the way
i loved you.

all i can do is write a rhyme

because it's all you understand.
when every thought slips & turns to sand,
swallows me up & blurs me out, there is only
time, only doubt, of everything i thought i felt:
the love, the eyes, but it's all gone now, watch it
melt to demise. that's what existence is when
there is no support. no one looking out
to witness me fall apart. see me kneel on the
ground praying & wishing it won't be per diem,
it is only the steam washing out of my system.
it is only one night that i feel this alone.
only one moment that there's a dial tone
in place of your voice, in place of your smell.
why is it that i care too much? i care to tell
i feel alone every night i'm in bed? these nights
i wish i had said, "come stay with me, come stay
instead. come stay & forget about raps, forget
about maps of places you've never been
because you're here now
& there's nothing that can change that."
in the world there is nothing to count on.
no one who will stay til dawn. no one who will
fuck just me or care about things they can't see.
what lies in my heart is more than one can
fathom, in every second there is purpose,
there is passion. because i know what it's like

to want to be someone else. i know what it's like
to look at a sharp knife & wonder how deep
it's going to cut me next time i'm not coping
with the fear & loathing. the next time i see you
with another bitch. the next time i might need a
needle & stitch, a rope & a ditch, a candlestick
or a wrench to finish me off, it's already begun.
all i want is to be understood, to know i could,
if only i could have a voice, have a chance, have
the next dance with you in the harbored
trance of a morning rain, on a faraway coast in a
weathered freight. all i want is some permanent
damage to know i'm alive & scars to prove every
day i strived to make something better than
myself. in place of this void. in the battered
remnants of some hollow resistance. in existence
to my thousands of forgotten prayers said again &
again to a burning god in the childhood words of
a scared little girl. "send angels to surround me,
protect me from this dark." (but god, oh god, can
you protect me from myself?)
all i can do is write a rhyme because tomorrow
you won't understand & neither will i, waking
with a belly of cheap tequila in a bed of lies. this
is one of many late nights. one of many drunken
raps. one too many cigarettes burned the wrong
way. one of the times i feel abandoned. one
person that disassembled my heart. one
of many times i fall asleep looking at the stars
wondering if there will ever be less than <
a million miles between us.

escape ladders

1. hydrant sprays sheets on hot corners.
hair trimmings caught flame in a three-story
apartment where a psychic cut hair for free.
she enjoyed the company & metal scissors
over cobalt sinks.
she built herself from the wiring down.
must have been freon, hairspray, or polish
remover placed against a hot iron or an open
socket. lit the drapes & mothers were caught
inside, their curlers locked together. the psychic
threw her cat, favorite book, & a few paintings out
the window before pushing the mass of widows
down the fire escape. they all had minor burns
& smoke stains.

2. one charred widow tells me that when she lived
on this block, she carried a pocket knife.
walked home alone at night, used it to break into
an abandoned house where she set fire to pages
of journals so her mother couldn't read them.
cut a man she saw every day sitting against the
courthouse. one night he decided to pick her up,
sling her over his shoulder. the girl scout brigade
blade stuck like cursive acupuncture. it gave her
time to run. she wrote a script on the experience,
claims the production studios are drunk on the
story.

3. i walk home through an empty mall.
neon gleam no movement inside consumer-land.
silence penetrates chain stale windowed bodies.
dinosaur grease burns off restaurant rooftops.
i flip the pocket knife as waitresses file out,
drive across town to apartments where some find
fire trucks. i wish the pavement would burn, not
nail polish, journals, hair, but this place
is invincible.
without escape
ladders.

4. the psychic claimed to have seen the ghost
of a man rise out of bubbling curlers.
firefighters assured her, "just smoke."
she knew it was her brother who died
thirty years ago, she, a girl in charleston.
one night he drove his motorcycle over three
mile, disappeared. some say it was suicide.
she wanted her kids strong like him,
named them stone cold, & steve austin.
they had to walk everywhere, yellow petal weeds
pressed downstream on their knees,
crossing into odessa to buy milk & eggs.
i witnessed their widowed mother watch
the three-story apartment burn to the ground.
she wondered if it was a sign.
she told me that all she had forseen
was the motorcycle plummeting.

october

there is a deepness, an emptiness every october.
i am too alive when the cold leaks in through
the cracks. when i get this feeling i am alone
even in a crowd. i try to fill the sinking void
with affection. this is when i get attached
to warmth. this is when i go a little crazy
for sick attention. walk alone at night
along the train tracks. the stench of metal
lights, the natural cycle of death, & there is
happiness in being a recluse in dim furrows
of leaves. a wild spirit frees from my body &
i dissociate. all the things i see are not mine,
all the words i write are detached. something
blooms where everything else shrivels. something
opaque & real, realer than fiction reels.
something that stalks me in the pure daylight,
is not afraid to show its face & breasts open
& free, reflecting my trapped shell
of a self conscious.
heartland shoves a dress on me, mindful
of what identity comes next, insignificant ticket
to hells i couldn't even conjure. what really
matters is buried beneath hills of blue collars,
buried beneath towers sending cell phone
reception, buried beneath expectations of
product distribution.

a shallow pond drained. all the fish left in the sun.

how can i tap into what is real?
how can i tap into you?
i could dig whatever is left & lie it out,
but in the depth there is warmth & damp soil.
bury myself inside & rest there for awhile.
the wind is too cold. i need a sleeping bag
of realness to wrap frozen hands. a sleeping bag
full of your dirt, all you can dig up.
if there is one faceless cloud, let it snow & bury
me deeper bellow the surface of a designer world.
this designed antique toy of existence.
will you hide with me or continue to breathe
manufactured air? will you travel the train tracks
until you find me & my shovel?
if not, then i will rise from the ground in spring,
blooming while the world shrivels in on itself.

cats eye hazel lakes

i never want to say sorry again
unless i crush your heart. even then-
the river, the leaves, the vortex spins.
i want nothing from you.
the silence is perfect enough,
mere presence of beauty fills me up.
tip me over into your cup.
there you observe the anogenesis
of my love: the grasping & letting go
of self again & again. it's cyclical
& with every autumn i die & move on.
the wind pass lifts my dead cells, spells,
prayers for rebirth, for cladogenesis:
all-encompassing wave, particle,
signal you can sense.
when i peer on the marble surface
of your cat's eyes hazel lakes,
there's an iceberg of imaginary states.
its movement uncharted, of free will.
it skates with candle across melting
tides & i can't contain them,
no reason to try.
there will remain mystery (my story)
in the blinking brights of your eyes.
sometimes i'm just afraid of infinity
contained, the tightly packaged miles of dna.
sometimes language of mortals can't say,
can't express nearly anything

like one flash from you,
one strand of protein,
written synthesis
[mitosis]
[meiosis]
[music].
juncture of a spiritual intervention,
this gray matter is from the seventh dimension.
there are no coincidences.
you are the antecedence
& i am your audience.
so never say sorry again.
unless you crush my heart.
even then.

druid arch

the wind is powerful here.
the heat.
the isolation.
- the onset of paranoia -
let it go with the wind.
a crow watches us.
a raven soars through the canyon.
the maze surrounds us.
the fierce beauty of this place
makes me remember to trust.
trust spirit guides & know
i have propulsion in this life
like none other before it.

nothing lives out here. it's silent.
this sacred dry oasis that used to be
the bottom of an ocean.
the salt deposits eroded the sandstone.
i visualize snails, crabs, starfish, sharks
swimming in the crevices.
the energy of the ocean resides within these walls
that once felt waters engulf & caress them.
now the wind echoes the surf.

the story of this place is cosmically beautiful.
billions of years have passed in a time lapse.
the greater artist used gravity, wind, water,
forces of nature as a medium.

this something somewhere that had a say,
shaping every landscape & beings to interact.
brush strokes down the canyon,
blue whales swimming.
needles sticking straight up into the sky.

we are one with this landscape.

wild flowers blooming in the harshest
environment. a plant system with virtually no
water, surviving on cryptobiotic soil, minerals &
salt. there is no escape from fear, never run &
hide, always face it, but don't look it straight in the
eye. the power of nature is beating down up us,
even in our modern attempt to destroy it.

we must love nature, & therefore stop trying to
adapt her. we must accept all pain & all death
so that fear doesn't control us.

(this planet will win over those
who attempt to destroy it.)

walking through the valley

of boulder this day, after dreams of a psychic scene, can never say what i really mean to them lest i insult the majority fission who scrap their vision for a sip of moonshine to escape. you can't scape goat the rape of the debtor's prison, they cut our umbilical cords, & put chains on our physical forms. invisible debts of each child born, what's their price on the marketplace? babylon selling human slaves, disguising it as free trade. we can't escape, but we can ascend. think modernity is great? well look again: the trash in the creek, the cars on the street, the pollution we breathe. i can't take it.

soon the planet will thrust a spear at the heart of the beast we're inside, struggling to survive- to break apart greedy capitalism. lets recognize the victims, children dying while some spend billions on stupid shit. let's not celebrate until everyone has a full plate. is this error of economics or have humans lost compassion? world peace & ending hunger is a heart reaction. it's within our reach if everyone give up their luxuries for once in all, all for one.

it's not invisible anymore who's killing the planet that only gave us life. that's why we must end this strife & fight only cease the battles in the valley of

the shadow of death. i fear no evil, for thou art
with me- a sword of truth sheathed inside,
a gemstone forged by fire, songs that speak of
ancient streams of knowledge, songs that speak of
greater then self, beyond this moment. spirit
guides please recognize my face as a protector of
the planet. cause there is still hope for us walking
through the valley, after dreams of psychic scene.
sometimes it's worth saying what you really mean.

music is the past present future. music is
soundscape, mindscape, thoughtscape, emotion.
it's all powerful to move mountains.

our cells are vibrating, every one of them.
our cells are responding to the universe in song.

god is not a man in the sky. god is a state of mind.
my thought is not my own, they're shared by all,
so let go of control.

goddess is not a deity in the myth. goddess is
constant bliss. this song is not my own,
they come & go.
so no more ego.

hollow place

church & state is a blind date.
unwind them quick, so they can't mate.
i am the shy calling out the demise
of a system so awry it's ignorant
to the fourteen billion eyes that can see
there is something beyond this so called reality.
but can you see me?
what's inside?
advantage from the third eye:
clairvoyance, telepathy. indigo children
will rise from hypocrisy of war on terror.

ALL WAR IS TERROR.

so open up the senses to a meditative rate,
seek truth every second, minute, day.
a mantra is powerful enough to grant us
a wish if given the trust, so trust me,
not our government, military, or tv.
we're at the cusp of paradigm shift
veil of aquarius lifts dust
off of the christ in us.

we were once two trees, two towers
growing on a river bank, overlooking
a sacred gate, another dimension.
we grew together for centuries, now
we've manifested as two human beings.

can grow together or apart.
nerve endings break for memories sake,
but let's not forget to hold the roots of earth
our mother at birth of a species so deviant
she took our powers away.
forsaken the moment
we turned against her for selfish gain.
dynamite the mountain for gold blocks,
mutate the seeds to grow gmo crops,
suck the oil from fossil remains,
pluck the trees for paper to waste,
animals shuffle in line for the slaughter,
this is not what mother wanted for her daughter!
to face the light of day with darkened thoughts
that truth lies beyond reach.
tell me that truth is within.
communicate love & teach peace.

IN WAR NOBODY WINS.

everything & nothing

everything exists & nothing exists.
within nothing is everything.
within everything is nothing.

i am nothing, no one, no identity,
no name, an animal wandering the earth.
i do not belong to myself & my made up self.
i do not belong to the earth.

i am everything, everyone, every identity,
every name, a human exploring the heavens.
i belong to myself & my self made me.
the heavens belong to me.

i am death dying to live.
every second i breath,
death creeps closer
to reclaim my mortal corpse.

i am life living to die.
every year i count, life
stretches further out
to release my immortal soul.

you see- i am you
i see- you are me.
the dark & light are one,
there is no distinction.

our eyes are wise,
but in split second we are blind.

i am the insect on the leaf,
basking in the sun.
i am the foot that breaks the leaf,
looking for shade.

my pain is finite.
my joy is infinite.
i am the universe, observing itself.
the universe is me, observing myself.

la isla del sol

"even the beloved, clear
stars look desolately down,
since i learned in my heart that
love can die." - herman hesse

smoke on the petal of a rose.
la isla del sol. the island of the sun.
in the eyes of a small bird,
reflection of a burning ember.
rose is grace with its stains
& discoloration. brown scars
in delicate ruby flesh.
bird is time with its tattered feathers,
tiny voice chirping in soundscape of waves.
in the grand scheme of earth,
mosquito eater has a wingspan
its presence is noted. its vibrations felt.
bundle of clouds that never end-
siempre en la distancia. *always in the distance.*
esta es la isla del sol. *this is the island of the sun.*
the purpose for the pain
is etched in our pupils.

doorway

doorway into an inner state
higher realms just a step away
energy has infinite shapes
yet we're made into a tetrahedron.
veil of isis drops from irises
cosmic mother, milky way
shows us her desired diadems
to dissolve dichotomy of sin.
goddess take us within
to where & when we first began
as an after thought, as a whim
begin a new age of human.
holding beautiful precious gems
that are conscious thoughts
whispered mantras into the wind
that have now finally been caught.
i find this peace within myself to overcome the
underworld------we will rise above until all
creation is living heaven-------------
stairway dna spiral light
reveals the fourth dimension-
black hole cells splinter into thoth.
single sound that spoke the universe
the same sound radiates freeing
soul from body, a spiritual being
emerges
skywalker of the stars, take your place
among your brothers,

sisters with the same face.
don't hold onto the physical plane.
we'll spend eternity
making love at lights pace.
pure energy exploring
billions of galaxies in space.
don't hold back, don't implode
set in motion, was your potential
now is time to use the power you hold,
show the world that love is influential.

counter attack

counter attack with white magic,
summon forgotten knowledge
from thousands of lives which i fought,
endless battles & for what?
to get to this very spot, now a clear horizon.
this generation must protect free thought,
mend wounds that are starting to rot,
heal from this millennia old hate,
come together despite age, sex, or race,
dispel the negative before it's too late.
i must become the white mage-
cast spells to block the warlocks,
build community in our broken state,
rise above in unity & admit to my mistakes.
that's what makes a coward into hero:
striving to become a better self, in order to shake
the numb people awake.
stir the cauldron- turn tears,
transfuse blood into music of the spheres.
for planet's sake- counter with white magic,
end this jealous rage & give into fate.
cause what was meant to be will be my love
so let me free & i will be the one
to release you from your disbelief
that magic is real & love is powerful.
i'm here for you in all walks of this treacherous
life, we build each other up, take my hand.
i will see you for you

not in the projection of me,
but as the goddess trinity.
you can heal yourself
just believe in love.
you can heal yourself
create & cast white spells.
i can heal myself,
here is my musical spell.
we can heal the world
here is our white spell...

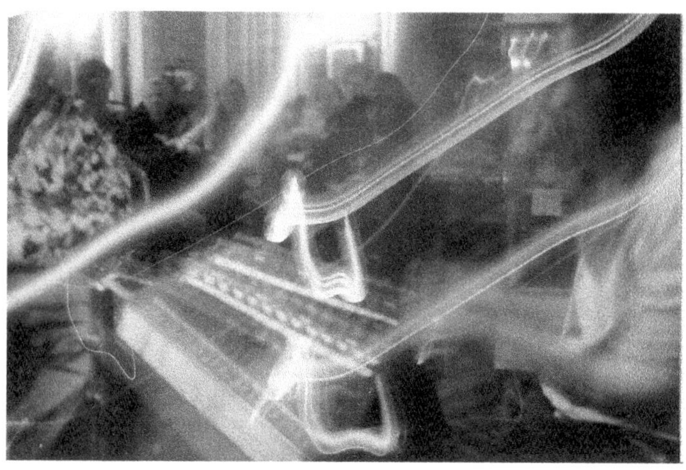

lone wolf

i am extemporaneous colliding with solicitude &
solitude. i speak too much truth with not enough
words. but images, like truth, are subjective.
whittled wood into a flute, painted it with sunset,
red burning joy of creation.
i play on the crag of a canyon, on the edge of the
city- see a lone coyote in the distance, yipping to
the others not to follow. there is nothing this way
but a wasteland of asphalt & speeding trucks- a
highway that never stops. an endless cycle of
consumers, polluters, & piston shooters.
the violent shadow rises as the sun falls below the
walls of the deserted canyon. my spirit restive-
impatient, uneasy, it wants to fly.
sick of prolixity. chained to misconceptions.
yet plenary, complete unto itself.
the body is full of fear, yet courageous.
climbing when there is risk of fall... it is our spirits
that help us go on in spite of intense fear.
anneal- the body, the mind, the spirit- set it on
fire. dose it in snow. boil it in flames. wash it with
white water. cleanse the limpid with hot & cold.
coat the translucent with blood, sweat, tears-
to construct a soul- not a façade.
does the lone wolf wear a mask?
it is the arcana. its intuitive freedom lies within its
ability to take full responsibility for its existence,
for its well being, for its survival, for the
continuation of life. does the lone coyote turn

back or take the road to the city & rummage the
dumpsters for scraps? the alternative is a long hot
desert hall, with perhaps no food or water. does
the human species survive alone? no- we depend
on each other to evolve- our own perceptions,
our systematic codex, our subjective filtered
mediated legitimacy. perhaps there is no truth,
then why, am i writing this? if there is no truth
there is no point to existence there is no self------
so there must be at least one truth. one goal. one
root of all desire. one tree of knowledge, one
fountain of youth, one elixir of love, one vile
bottle of jealous poison, one structure of creation,
one tablet of cuneiform that contains a microbe
of truth. truth that is not transient, but innate.
the canyon was once a warm ocean.
the mountains were once a coast.
the native never stayed here.
for it is too sacred.
the spirits pass through the egress.
the clouds roll over the hills & into the valley
strewn with boulders from the chaos.
once upon a time titans ruled this land,
giants who threw these boulders like stones.
they lived until the pain of their hunger
outweighed the glory of the tribe.
they had to shrink to survive, melt down to a
reasonable size. their spirits still remain- they float
as elephants in the clouds to reclaim the ancient
daze, sitting atop the flatirons in a purple haze.

smoking enormous bowls from colossal apex
colas of the magic variety.
now our bodies are small,
but our spirits remain as nephalim, seraphim,
titans, bohemic behemoths- nomads on the arid
prairie, cookin' up mythology about the stars. our
spirits are strong. stronger than our bodies,
stronger than our minds they continue on even
after death, after time passes quicker & quicker-
the one truth remains. & within the lone wolf,
the lone coyote, the lone owl-
the song of the one truth rings forth
through the red rock walls- their cells
reverberate, vibrate, & hum with the frequency.
despite the fact that humans are flawed
& we have no one true love, the one essential
truth is love. it is the conclusion, the goal, the
object of perpetual desire. i keep arriving
back to it over & over, it is the constant among
the constant change all around,
encasing it in pain & beauty & hardship
& struggle & joy & fear & every emotion that is
possible to feel, label, & categorize.
love does not fit into our tiny neatly wrapped
boxes. it does not run dry, if we reach into the
well inside.
there is no word that could ever describe the
magic of when two souls collide,
make love in the desert sun among wildflowers
that continue to bloom despite the drought &
despite the odds against them, they still find each

other, the loner finds a friend, the friend finds a
lover, the lover finds a soul mate.
this is the unending desire
& we, the lone wolves, continue on...

11.11.11

prophet of the new age emerges,
circumnavigating dark water
she's on the verge of,
throwing paint in the sky
& look at what's scribed on her heart:
chaotic abstract rendered artless.
colors remit the present intense.
she bleeds nonexistence into earth,
tells of rebirth, wrapped the cord
around her head & should be dead,
but was cut from womb & resurrected.
now she speaks on a box of inspiration,
reaches up to heaven & flings out creation,
a million sequins to light clouds.
she is a fire-starter, to burn the veil down,
conquer hell, find the key
to our slave cells set free.
though everything seems chaotic-
when we rise above,
it is the most sacred of geometry.
at the dawn of the eleventh sun
there will come voices on high,
harmonize our souls as one.
she says this is divine, don't be afraid
there's something cosmic on the day
11.11.11
it is a gateway.

prophet of the new age
indigo child with a bright face
smiles to change her space
in the world, to redeem herself
& find peace to give,
enjoy the love of friends,
raise goddess energy,
open to higher frequency,
resurrect natives of the grave,
recognize the prophets of the new age.
cosmic love is on the way.
11.11.11

she is isis & osiris in one,
virgin, mother, crone,
dark goddess of the moon,
shiva & brahma,
the twin two spirit,
mother & father,
a prophet never forgotten.
child & old woman
walking the earth barefoot,
without fear, without talking,
she says everything i need to hear.
cosmic love is on the way.
11.11.11
gateway

the feeling of time

undeniable wind penetrates pores, the open core. think twice before writing words, but words drip out as wax liquefies with fire. the fire of golden brilliance, true color of essential self. my heart further ignites & realizes it's own reflection. a fractured divinity, thrust into orbit of planetary gem. walking with infinite energy spiraling out, a human with two hands. hands of an artist. picking pennies off the street, for we are what we eat & i eat the moon, chew the glorious sun, drink the oceans of neptune. pen in mouth i spell out magic words. even if unfelt, the writer scribes the tale. the feeling of time. it issues from our mind. we are no hollow shell. we create a central point & magnetically attract objects in accordance.

find the space between
words & meaning.
the space between moments
passing. find the fox.

my skin falls off my face & light breaks from within. glowing orb that has surrounded itself with yin & yin is to envision what we could do with our intuitive wisdom. watching the birds, the ducks swim; i pray for unconditional love. for the breaking point. watching myself watching the birds, i become a higher self almost ascending this world. activating star points, i connect with the eternal passing. the feeling of time brings me

back into body. i am not mine. i do not possess a
self. i am a puzzle piece, the corner: knowing i
have a purpose, yet not fitting in with the others.
this is the time. yet everyone is still enthralled
with illusion, controlled by screens, &
manipulated with religious jargon. they peak out
from soul windows & see the birds, but perhaps,
they do not see themselves seeing the birds-
flocks with feathers tattered & torn, they cannot
see themselves as the birds, with potential to fly.

i touch stars.   as i touch you.
& though you cannot love me the same,
i do not regret feeling this.

feeling the time pass slow.

i am impatient.
feeling the time pass quick. i am ancient.

secret brew

why are the most beautiful things in life the most
hidden? kept in secret places, the gemstones.
comforted in darkness, shrouded & invisible.
but beauty must be shared, or else, wither.
beauty must be seen. or why, then,
is it in our midst?
the most beautiful things in life are the most
hidden. they are the most scarred. the most
abused. the most sacred, yet resistant to
openness.
you are open.
somehow,
beyond all attempts to destroy beauty,
take it away from you.
you are innocent.
somehow,
through the abuse, the pain.
you are alive. beneath life, trickling up like a
spring. something remains hidden, under rocks
that cut. hidden eggs of confidence. hidden
acceptance. pain & pleasure the same. life &
death a congruent moment, with no time in-
between. we are here in pain/pleasure,
life/death, here together.
innocent wanderer, adolescent,
birthed again in this life for love,
to discover it's form & function,
to write intense poems, to express desire;

as a human, as a goddess, as a catalyst, as a
novice, as an elder, as a teacher, as a student of
the universe, embodying courage
to love.
& what could ever be more painful?
show me the beauty that is hidden.
through your sense of self illusive,
love slams you against the shoreline.
this is it.
you. naked, rolled in sand.
hair dreaded & strewn with seaweed,
an anomaly. vulnerable outsider, outcast, lone
traveler of the past. from another planet, crash-
landed, misunderstood, misrepresented, under-
appreciated. this is you, hollow, yet so dam full.
a once forgotten song, forgotten tale. a poet with
no metaphors, a musician with no theory, a writer
who doesn't read. hiding in the shadows, but
doesn't want to be alone. each one of us, a vessel,
wishing to connect, wanting to fill each other's
emptied cups.
you have no liquid left, all the blood drained.
you've been abandoned in the sun.   but
you are not done. you are not done.
yes, your heart is a quahog. a clam without a
shell. an oyster with no pearl. it has been stolen
from everyone who wants something from you,
but doesn't want you.
you are still open.
underneath the facade,
underneath the persona,

an artist lost,
a bodhisattva slipping back into samsāra.
beauty & the beast in one body, clutch the dying
rose, so that thorns draw blood. magician torn
between genders, bending definitions, traversing
dimensions. you will never quit this, accept that
yes, you are different. but there are others out
there like you. they write synonymous words, &
wonder who will reject them, who will protect
them, who will love them. no, not untouchable.
not excluded from heaven, not denied friendship.
unconventional, eccentric, witch. you are the
symbol of how to persist, throw off insults, stares,
& gossip everywhere you go, just because you
show who you really are.
a planet
rests on your forehead.
a field of horses.
a beach at the base of your heel.
a shell of light.

return
to this poem
to heal.
open
the door
to vast amounts
of beauty within.
within your caverns,
that i can never explore.
you could give me a taste,

but even that is too intoxicating.
a secret brew that's been ruminating
for lifetimes. stirred & sipped,
spiced & savored.

imitation

spirit as imitation.
child imagination
thrives on caress.
electrons outlined
fireflies caught
in well of an hourglass.
no thing to hold,
no blankets only opaque cloud.
spirit as imitation. hold onto heaven
as it slips out the back door.
hush. listen. the whistle.
train issues spirits to return.
i'm uncertain
as if i should go.
if i am human,
i am mere imitation.
honey on star lips
when birthed ajar
are not meant to be shut.
return artificial intellect for innocence.
i see fields of resonance, cells sojourn untouched.
or are they all spliced into filmic nostalgia?

simulated memory
fabricated herstory
synthetic phases
of my childhood.

in the hands of this child
something timeless: a spiral strand,
a wand, a sword, a gold cup, a stone.
do we create everything
we touch? or is [it]
an imitation?

love slams me against the shoreline.
this is it.
me. naked. rolled in sand...

red | book poems
poetry & visual art

åsalott
(allison lotterhos)

◊ dream-jungle press ◊

www.ingramcontent.com/pod-product-compliance
Ingram Content Group UK Ltd.
Pitfield, Milton Keynes, MK11 3LW, UK
UKHW020217250726
13967UKWH00001B/41

9 781300 593287